I0797356

HOW TO MEASURE

Volume

Beth Bence Reinke

3.4 fl oz

8.5 fl oz

LIGHTBOX
openlightbox.com

Lightbox is an all-inclusive digital solution for the teaching and learning of curriculum topics in an original, groundbreaking way. Lightbox is based on National Curriculum Standards.

STANDARD FEATURES OF LIGHTBOX

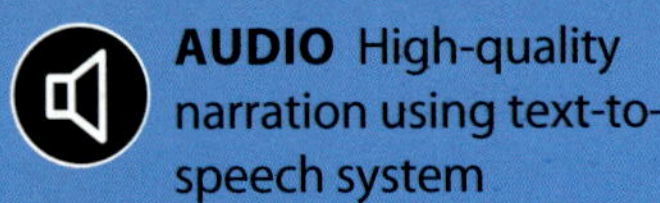

AUDIO High-quality narration using text-to-speech system

ACTIVITIES Printable PDFs that can be emailed and graded

SLIDESHOWS Pictorial overviews of key concepts

VIDEOS Embedded high-definition video clips

WEBLINKS Curated links to external, child-safe resources

TRANSPARENCIES Step-by-step layering of maps, diagrams, charts, and timelines

INTERACTIVE MAPS Interactive maps and aerial satellite imagery

QUIZZES Ten multiple choice questions that are automatically graded and emailed for teacher assessment

KEY WORDS Matching key concepts to their definitions

Contents

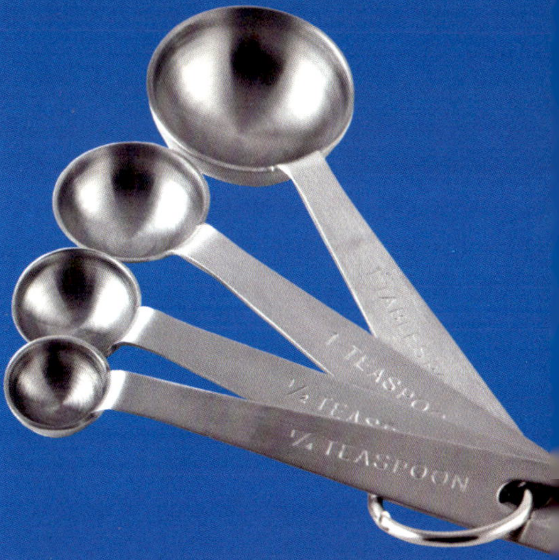

What Is Volume?

You can fill the bathtub with water. Or you can pour juice into a glass. You can scoop sand into a bucket, too.

Juice has a lot of sugar. Kids should drink less than one glass of juice a day.

Kids should drink about two glasses of milk a day. That is enough to fill two baseballs.

Look at a glass of milk. Can you tell how much is in it? It's hard to know just by looking. You can measure the milk to find the **volume**. Volume is how much space something takes up. Everything big and small has volume.

The word "**volume**" comes from the 14th-century French word *volum*, which means "scroll" or "**book**."

The lake with the **largest volume** in the world is Lake Baikal in Russia.

Jupiter has the **largest volume** of all the planets in the solar system.

How much water is in a swimming pool? How much ketchup does the bottle hold? How much milk and cereal are in your bowl? You can find out. Let's measure volume!

To do the activities in this book, you will need:

- **measuring cup**
- measuring spoons
- dry rice or unpopped popcorn
- **funnel**
- empty **gallon** jug
- empty quart bottle
- empty **liter** bottle

Volume Timeline

3000 BC The Babylonians and Egyptians fill containers with plant seeds, then count the seeds to measure the containers' volumes.

900 BC To measure the volumes of food and drink, the Greeks use pots of set sizes. Water, olives, grains, and other items each have a specially sized pot.

200s BC The Greek **mathematician** and inventor Archimedes comes up with different ways to find the volumes of shapes, such as spheres and cylinders.

400–1200 AD Many different systems, or ways, of measuring volume are in use around the world. This becomes confusing when different countries want to trade food and drink.

1668 Scientist John Wilkins of Great Britain writes an important essay. He says the entire world needs to use the same measurements for volume.

2017 People and businesses can now use laser devices to measure large volumes. A system of lasers can map and measure volumes of materials in different sized containers. The system then sends the information to laptop computers or cell phones.

Volume Big and Small

Everything has volume. What if you have something big to measure? You need big **units** of volume. We use gallons or liters for water in a swimming pool. Gallons and liters are units of measure for liquids. Small amounts need small units. We use teaspoons or milliliters for medicine.

To measure the volume of a liquid, a scientist might use a container called a graduated cylinder.

This chart will help you remember units of volume.

1 gallon	4 quarts	3.8 liters
1 quart	2 pints	0.9 L
1 pint	2 cups	0.5 L
1 cup	8 fluid ounces	0.2 L
1 fluid ounce	2 tablespoons	30 milliliters
1 tablespoon	3 teaspoons	15 mL

When food or drink is broken up into different volumes, it is called portioning.

Look at a container of ice cream and a container of milk. Which has a greater volume? One is taller than the other. They are not the same shape. One might be heavier, too. But their volume is the same. The two containers take up the same amount of space.

Ice cream and milk often come in the same volumes: pints, quarts, half-gallons, and gallons.

Activity

Measuring Ingredients

Instructions:

1. Measure these amounts of dry rice or unpopped popcorn. As you measure, dump them into a big bowl.
   - 2 cups (same as 1 pint)
   - 1 cup (same as 8 fluid ounces)
   - 2 tablespoons (same as 1 fluid ounce)
   - 3 teaspoons (same as 1 tablespoon)
2. Put the food back into the box when you are finished.

Choosing Units

Ava is having friends over to play. She is making snacks to serve.

What food shall Ava give her friends? Ava wants to make a snack mix. She has peanuts, pretzels, raisins, and cereal squares.

Cooks use volume, as well as weight, to measure out food.

One cup (0.2 L) of each ingredient adds up to four cups total, or one quart (0.9 L).

Ava will make a quart of snack mix. A quart is a unit of measurement. One quart is two pints (0.9 L). Each pint is two cups (0.5 L).

That means one quart has four cups. Ava needs four cups of snack mix. There are four **ingredients**. She will use one cup (0.2 L) of each.

Ava used cups to make the snack mix. Now she wants to add cinnamon. She needs a smaller unit of measurement.

Fluid ounces are small. There are eight fluid ounces in a cup (0.2 L). Tablespoons and teaspoons are even smaller. A tablespoon (15 mL) of butter melts in a frying pan. A teaspoon (5 mL) of vanilla goes in cookie batter.

When cooking, accurate measurements can be important. Too much or too little of an ingredient can ruin a dish.

Activity

Choose Your Units

Which units of volume could be used to measure these things? Copy this chart on to a piece of paper and fill it in. One unit is filled in for you.

Food for a kitten: tablespoons..

Cough medicine in a bottle:..

Paint for the walls:..

Cinnamon in a recipe: ....

Shampoo in a bottle:..

Water in a swimming pool: ....

Sand in a sandbox: ....

Juice for a snack: ....

Other Ways to Measure

On average, kids drink twice as much milk as adults.

Jack is thirsty! He has a gallon of milk. A gallon is a unit in the **U.S. customary system**. There are four quarts in a gallon (3.8 L).

Jack is making punch, too. The recipe uses quarts and liters. A liter is a bit bigger than a quart. You can buy two-liter bottles of soda at the store. The liter is a unit in the **metric system**. A shorter way to write liter is L. The metric system is another way to measure. It uses different units than the standard U.S. system. Milliliters are another unit in the metric system. There are 1,000 milliliters in a liter. A shorter way to write milliliter is mL.

A two-liter bottle of cola contains more than one cup (0.2 L) of sugar.

The average American drinks almost **40 gallons** (150 L) of **soda** a year.

The United States, Liberia, and Myanmar are the only **three** countries that do not use the **metric system**.

The world record for **largest iced tea** is **2,524 gallons** (9,554 L).

Jack has two glasses. One glass is tall and narrow. One is short and wide. Can you guess which glass holds more punch?

Jack fills each glass with punch. He pours the punch from each glass into a measuring cup. Both glasses hold the same amount! Volume can be tricky. It is hard to guess how much liquid there is. That is why we measure instead of guessing.

People often think short, wide glasses have less liquid in them than tall, narrow glasses.

Activity

Fill a Jug

Instructions:

1. Gather three sizes of empty bottles: a gallon, a quart, and a liter.
2. First, place a funnel in the top of the gallon jug.
3. Then use the quart bottle to fill the gallon jug with water. How many quarts do you use to make a gallon?
4. Next, use the liter bottle to fill the gallon jug. Did the last liter fit? Which has more volume, a quart or a liter?

About 30 percent of the glass containers used for food and drink in the United States are recycled after use.

Record-Setting Volumes

There are many record-setting landmarks in the United States. Some of these have the largest volumes in the nation, or even in the world.

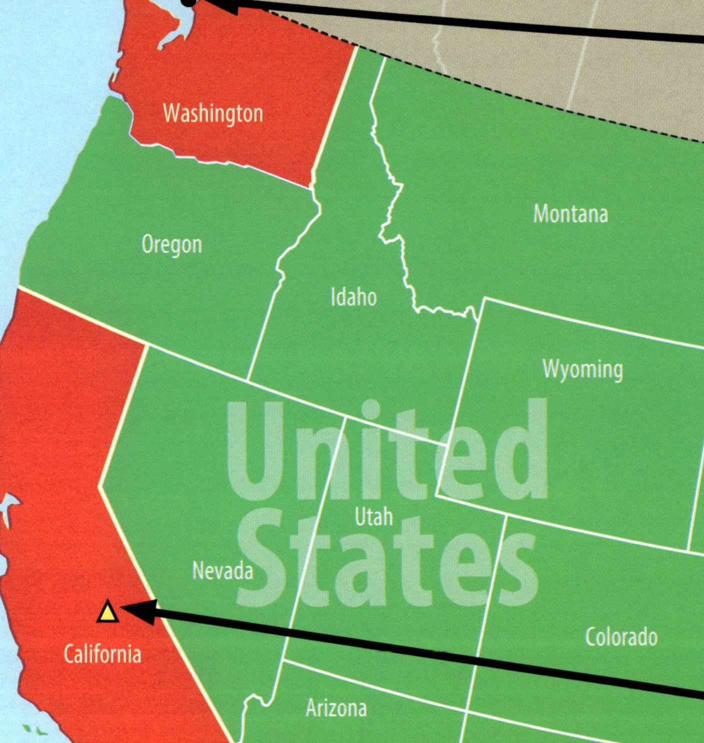

Pacific Ocean

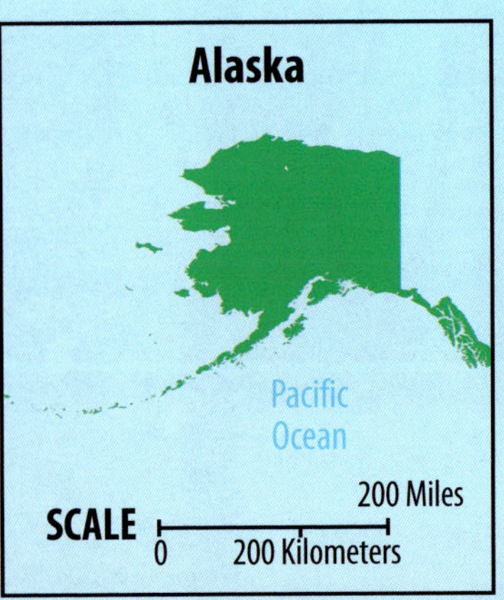

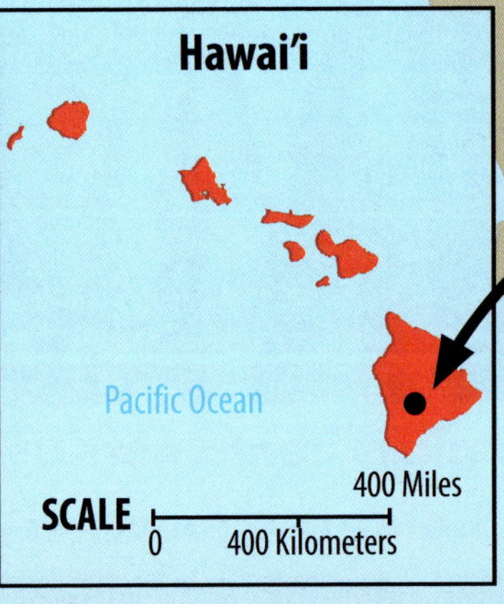

Mauna Loa
South Kona, Hawai'i
In terms of volume, Mauna Loa is the largest volcano on Earth. Scientists estimate it is 9,600 cubic miles (40,000 cubic kilometers).

Boeing Everett Factory
Everett, Washington
The Boeing airplane factory in Washington state is one of the largest buildings in the world. It has a volume of 472 million cubic feet (13.3 million cubic meters).
Lake Superior
Great Lakes
Lake Superior is the lake with the largest volume in the United States. Its volume is estimated at 3 quadrillion gallons (11 quadrillion L).
Sequoia National Park
California
A giant sequoia named General Sherman is the largest tree in the world. It has a volume of 52,500 cubic feet (1,500 cubic m).
North Dakota
Minnesota
South Dakota
Wisconsin
Michigan
New York
Maine
Vermont
New Hampshire
Massachusetts
Rhode Island
Connecticut
Pennsylvania
New Jersey
Delaware
Maryland
Ohio
West Virginia
Virginia
North Carolina
South Carolina
Atlantic Ocean
Arkansas
Texas
Mississippi
Alabama
Georgia
Louisiana
Florida
LEGEND
United States
Other Countries
Lake Superior
Water
City
National Park
SCALE
0
250 Miles
250 Kilometers
N
S
E
W

Quiz

1 Which planet has the largest volume?

2 What units are used for measuring water in a swimming pool?

3 What might scientists use to measure the volume of liquids?

4 How many quarts are in a gallon?

5 How many teaspoons are in a tablespoon?

6 How do cooks measure out food?

7 What is a shorter way to write liter?

8 Does the United States use the metric system?

9 Which lake has the largest volume in the United States?

10 Where is the largest tree in the world located?

Answers: 1. Jupiter **2.** Gallons or liters **3.** A graduated cylinder **4.** 4 **5.** 3 **6.** By volume and weight **7.** L **8.** No **9.** Lake Superior **10.** Sequoia National Park, California

Key Words

funnel: a hollow cone with a tube pointing down to direct flow into a small hole

gallon: a unit of volume used in the U.S. customary system and equal to 16 cups (3,785 mL)

ingredients: the parts of a mixture

liter: a unit of volume used in the metric system and equal to 1,000 milliliters (4.2 cups)

mathematician: a person with great skill at math

measuring cup: a cup made of glass, metal, or plastic with markings of volume, used for measuring ingredients when cooking

metric system: a way to measure things based on the number ten; the liter is used to measure volume

units: standard amounts that are used to measure things

U.S. customary system: units of measurement most often used in the United States such as cups, quarts, miles, feet, and inches

volume: the amount of space an object takes up

Index

LIGHTBOX

SUPPLEMENTARY RESOURCES

Click on the plus icon ⊕ found in the bottom left corner of each spread to open additional teacher resources.

- Download and print the book's quizzes and activities
- Access curriculum correlations
- Explore additional web applications that enhance the Lightbox experience

LIGHTBOX DIGITAL TITLES
Packed full of integrated media

VIDEOS

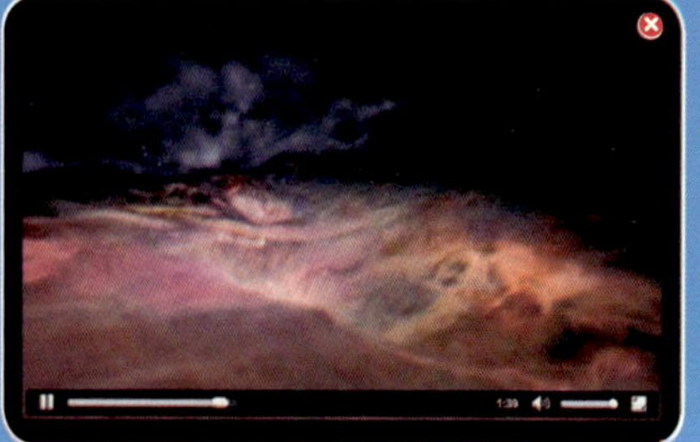

INTERACTIVE MAPS

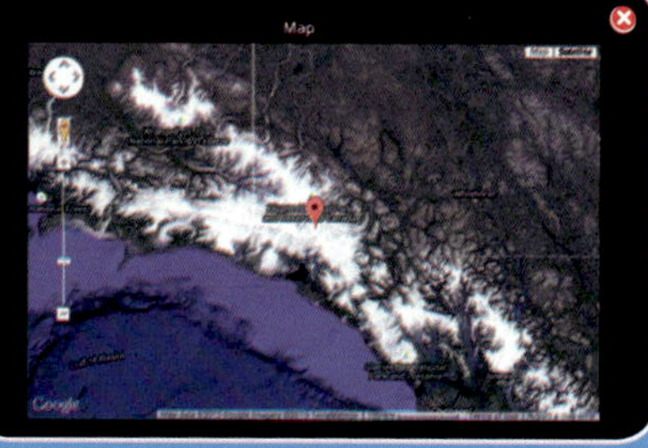

WEBLINKS

SLIDESHOWS

QUIZZES

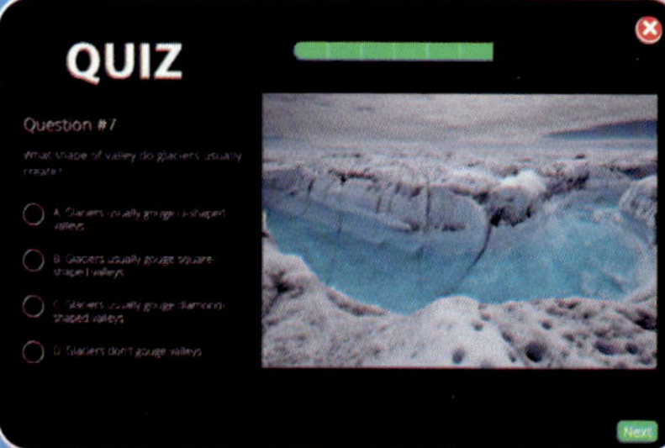

OPTIMIZED FOR

- ✓ TABLETS
- ✓ WHITEBOARDS
- ✓ COMPUTERS
- ✓ AND MUCH MORE!

Published by Smartbook Media Inc. 350 5th Avenue, 59th Floor New York, NY 10118
Website: www.openlightbox.com

012018
120517

Library of Congress Control Number: 2017960154

ISBN 978-1-5105-3636-4 (hardcover)
ISBN 978-1-5105-3637-1 (multi-user eBook)

Printed in the Brainerd, Minnesota, United States
1 2 3 4 5 6 7 8 9 0 22 21 20 19 18

First published by Cherry Lake in 2014.

Project Coordinator: John Willis
Designer: Ana María Vidal

Every reasonable effort has been made to trace ownership and to obtain permission to reprint copyright material. The publisher would be pleased to have any errors or omissions brought to its attention so that they may be corrected in subsequent printings.

The publisher acknowledges Alamy, Getty Images, Shutterstock, and iStock as the primary image suppliers for this title.